STYLING NATURE

STYLING NATURE

A Masterful Approach to Floral Arrangements

Lewis Miller

With Irini Arakas

Photography by Don Freeman

Foreword by Nina Garcia

RIZZOLI
NEW YORK

New York · Paris · London · Milan

CONTENTS

Like passages from Proust, my images resonate with memory, evoking the touch of the soft light of an early morning, nostalgia for happiness or love, or visions of another world where time has stood still. I have always loved photographing flowers and trying to give them a life that will remain long after they are gone—saved from oblivion.

I began this journey of documenting Lewis's work over a decade ago. His style brings to mind an old-world charm, but with a passion for what's new and modern. I wanted these photographs to not only reference the past but also give us something that we can relate to today. This is a collaboration that is not so much built on nostalgia as it is a private exploration of an inner dimension of the mind that expresses music and poetry. By using simple sets and all-natural lighting, I hope these images paint a rich dreamscape that recalls a faded remembrance of beauty—simple rhythmic gestures, fragments of time that I hope we have not lost and can still enjoy.

I first encountered Lewis Miller's talents at the *Treasures from India: Jewels from the Al-Thani Collection* opening at the Metropolitan Museum of Art in 2014. Lewis's flowers for the event captivated me. Huge urns overflowed with plant life and bright green blossoms—bells of Ireland, hydrangeas, orchids, and green goddess calla lilies. There were giant displays of mixed flowers buzzing with life and animation. I was amazed at his fluency and fearlessness with the material and the manner in which he played with proportion and volume. The profusion of emerald green reminded me of my native Colombia. It is a visual memory that has stayed with me. This is what a true artist's work can do—transport you to a different place and elicit a powerful mood and feeling.

When I was asked to be a part of this beautiful book celebrating Lewis's talent and artistry, I sad *yes* most willingly. The weekly arrival of his flowers to my apartment is anticipated and enjoyed not only by me but also by my husband and children. The intricate and lush terrariums he architects for my sons bring out the childish enthusiasm in us all.

Simply put, Lewis designs on a higher plane than most, and his floral pairings are always unexpected and breathtaking. He is an iconoclast in his field. Never satisfied or conforming to a popular trend or style, he pushes boundaries—and himself—to make stunning work on his own terms. He has an artist's angst that never allows him to be entirely content with his finished pieces.

Lewis's arrangements are organically composed and always elegant. His floral designs retain that wild aspect that you find in nature, but they are always held together with control, style, and integrity. His flowers are full, robust, and sumptuous, with plenty of movement. At times oversized and out of proportion, blooms layered upon blooms, almost too big for the vase, spilling over and falling out. It is this mix of decadence—with just the right amount of chaos and definition—that appeals to me so much.

Working and living in New York City often separates one from a direct connection to nature, so to have Lewis's offerings in my home and to be able to admire the changing seasons through his work is an absolute blessing. In a similar way, this book allows his finest creations to be introduced into the homes of others who may not have the opportunity to experience his artistry firsthand. Nothing Lewis does looks or feels expected. There are so many layers and subtleties to his flower arrangements, and I would encourage the reader to appreciate and look at them the way one would admire an old-world painting.

B ooks written about flowers can be preachy and authoritative, packed with rules and complicated phrases describing techniques and the exact shade of red on the thin skin of a glistening wild berry. It is hard to write about flowers and not fall into that kind of trap. My hope is to have written a book that is expressive but also raw and soulful—not just for florists and creative professionals but for any flower lover who has the desire to bring flowers into his or her home and style them in a joyful and masterful way.

This book is comprised of still lifes made with flowers and plant life, beautiful vessels, and found objects photographed in various interiors. It's important for me to explain why I chose the word "masterful" (as some of you may raise an eyebrow to such a puffed-up word) and what I mean when I use it. I am inspired by many things that bring me great pleasure in their simplicity and order—English gardens, French potagers, even the uniform rows of tulips outside the bodega on the corner nearest my East Village office; but still-life paintings, especially works by the old Italian and Flemish masters, are some of my greatest sources of inspiration.

I love a still-life painting when the depiction is a fantasy conjured in the artist's mind. Deliberate choices are made; elements that might not share company in nature sit side by side on a candlelit table. A skillful, painterly hand brings disparate elements together, manipulates them for a moment in time, and captures the natural beauty of these living, vibrant things—and the result is authentic and timeless.

So how do we achieve this alchemy with flowers and floral arrangements? By breaking down a floral still life the way a painter would. Color, composition, movement, shape, and texture are the five basic principles to consider when creating a floral still life. Combining the descriptive with the practical, I have broken down these important themes into chapters and shared my knowledge, experience, and emotions with each one.

It is important to note that all of the arrangements in this book can be re-created. With the exception of one or two blooms, the flower material used in these arrangements can be purchased at a flower market. I did not pull the flowers from a fabulous garden or remote hothouse in the Netherlands. Nor are these specimens only available to me at a very particular moment in time. My relationship with flowers is similar to food. I dislike cookbooks in which a chef recounts recipes with mouthwatering images yet all of the ingredients are exotic and impossible to find. This is not my style. I do not forage the woods or spend years cultivating top-secret relationships with gardeners in faraway locations. These arrangements can be reproduced, and these flowers can be found in local flower markets.

My approach to floral design has always been a bit unorthodox. I see flowers in an unusual way, and I am happiest when I am combining opposing elements in my work. My aesthetic can go from monastic chic to the court of Versailles in the blink of an eye, and if sometimes I describe a flower as if it is an unruly teenager it's because all flowers are endowed with their own unique charms. The brilliant writer and garden designer Vita Sackville-West wrote: "I think that one should look at flowers in an imaginative way, to squeeze the fullest enjoyment from them." And I agree. When I look at a curved flowering almond branch, the sculpted back of a limber Martha Graham dancer comes into focus. A bouquet of perky tulips looks like a clutch of excited gospel singers in their Sunday best. Every flower, every plant has a personality. Celebrate them, imperfections and all. In the end, perfection is overrated and bores me to tears. It's the bumbles and imperfections in life—and in nature—that keep things interesting.

COLOR

I don't live with or wear much color—but my work is extremely colorful. Color is very important to setting a tone or a mood. Muddy or pure; crisp or muted; dark or light; rich or washed out—the nuances of colors in flowers are infinite. I prefer to work with bold, saturated colors. I love orange. Orange and yellow are two of my favorite colors. They work well with grays, blues, and darker blooms. My only real color dislikes are "Easter" pastels—unassertive lavenders, pinks, yellows, and greens.

I tend to like combinations of colors that either follow each other on the color wheel, like red, red-orange, and orange, or that fall on opposite sides of the wheel, like orange and blue. Successful color pairings are ones that have an unexpected twist, like coral with pink and rust, which is an alluring mix of hues. The rust is crucial in that trinity; without it the resulting floral arrangement is too sweet, it's as though your teeth will fall out just from looking at it! Salmon and olive; ruby, cerise, and coral; dusty lavender, aubergine, and champagne: these surprising combinations keep your eyes engaged and delighted.

IN THE BEGINNING, green, black, and white were the colors I worked with the most. I even wrapped my arrangements in black tissue paper. The visual impact, beauty, and strength of those three colors playing off each other were first revealed to me through director Peter Greenaway's film *The Draughtsman's Contract*. This film has had a huge impact on my work. It takes place at an English country manor and in its surrounding formal gardens. The servants wear black-and-white uniforms, and the landscaped trees cast long, dark shadows over the emerald-green lawns and hedges. The scenic composition and the contrasts between costume and nudity, nature and architecture swept me off my feet. There is a painterly approach to Greenaway's films that I respond to, and I approach working with color in a similar way.

Peter Greenaway, film still from *The Draughtsman's Contract* (1982)

I HAVE ALWAYS HAD A LOVE AFFAIR WITH GREEN. Geranium, peppermint, ivy, moss, grass, chartreuse, apple, and oak—no other color has such a strong connection to nature and to the earth. Green is life. Green is nutrition and energy. One of my first jobs in New York as a designer was at a large floral studio where the aesthetic was to tightly pack a vase with only flowers and to strip away any signs of foliage—those were dull floral days. My love of plants and leaves and herbs is a direct response to that time.

My first floral arrangement under my own name was called "The Jungle." It was an all-green arrangement—as in all greens, no flowers. It was the polar opposite of the arrangements I had to make while working for the other studio. It was lush, spiky, fuzzy, and herbal. It had texture and oozed life. It was my way of breaking away from the norm and blazing my own path, as no other floral designer at the time was creating all-green arrangements out of plant life and foliage. When I first started Lewis Miller Design (LMD) in 2002, I used materials to which I felt a deep connection; they happened to also be unorthodox and quite "taboo," yet I didn't think of what I was doing as "breaking the rules." Over a decade later, plant leaves and foliage are still integral to my work and often they upstage blooms and blossoms.

THERE IS SOMETHING SO RICH ABOUT BLACK FLOWERS. I find them quite uplifting. When I started my company, I had a running joke with my design team: if I came in feeling blue or stressed out, I would say, "I need something cheerful—make me a black arrangement." Truly, there is something about black basil or black scabiosa that makes me happy. When most people envision a black arrangement, the words "sinister," "funereal," or "Gothic" come to mind. But in the world of flowers, nothing is truly black. There are only shades of purple, red, and chocolate brown. When used together, the nuances of these dark colors and tones become apparent. Dark flowers and foliage can also act as "shadow" in an arrangement, knocking up against softer, brighter, and more colorful flowers.

I crave crisp edges, and I love a strong silhouette. I am drawn to and largely influenced by Gothic-style architecture and artists who use darkness in a similar way: the crosshatching of Edward Gorey, the easy lines of Hugo Guinness, and the silhouettes of Kara Walker, just to name a few.

In the French novel *Against Nature* by Joris-Karl Huysmans, the protagonist describes throwing a dinner party in which every component is black. The walls are sheathed in black taffeta. Ink pours out of the water fountains, coal covers the walkways, and violets are strewn about. The menu is also devoted to all things black. Caviar and tortoise soup are served to guests. It is one of the most delicious passages I have ever read, and it celebrates and echoes my love of all things dark and inky.

Hugo Guinness, *Florabunda I*

A table covered in raw canvas cloth and a series of clear glass bottles holding black flowers—that to me is the perfect summertime wedding. Some people would say dark flowers are for winter. But it's not about the black flowers—the arrangement is a living, breathing Hugo Guinness print and all you are meant to see is the shape.

I dislike the association of the word *Gothic* with horror, because Gothic to me is one of the most elegant styles, especially American Gothic. It has everything to do with the silhouette, the object. Whether it is a flower arrangement that is black, or an iron finial, a buttress, or a majestic tree, it's exclusively about the shape. That super elegant, sharp line, the cast of a shadow that is fanciful, powerful, and strong.

Pablo Picasso, *Trois Femmes* (*Three Women*) (1907–08)

Julian Schnabel, Pablo Picasso, Jackson Pollock: these are the artists who inspire me and inform my color choices. I like thick, wet-looking paintings. Paintings that appear dry and thirsty for paint have never held my attention. I want to see the energy of a brushstroke and the layers of paint and color on a canvas.

What I love about flowers and bringing color into the home through flowers is that they never outstay their welcome. It's a short-term relationship; after a few days you can find another color, another bloom, another arrangement to be bewitched by. These 'Maria Theresa' pink garden roses pop like graphic polka dots or bubble-gum bubbles that are just about to burst. You happily invite them into your home and into your life, but a week later—poof!—they are gone.

When making a floral arrangement, it is best not
to overthink the placement of the colors; thinking
too much about it will keep you from noticing the
serendipitous beauty of nature. The best way to
make an arrangement is to think about sex or
listen to one of your favorite songs while you're
creating the composition. Don't preoccupy yourself
with what colors are going where. Think about
something that you desire and trust your hands.

COMPOSITION

Flowers, when composed in a container or a vessel, become a floral arrangement. Take that arrangement and put it in a room. Consider the size of the flowers within their vessel and their proportions to the room and how they relate to the backdrop, the surface they are placed on, the neighboring elements, and their environment. This is composition; when you introduce fabric, curious objects, and lighting, you have a still life.

The anatomy of a floral still life is broken down into five categories: color, composition, movement, shape, and texture. Within all of these categories lies one common theme: duality.

Duality means contrast. Pairing something smooth with something rough. Mixing an exotic cattleya orchid with a common dahlia. Combining smooth galex leaves that reflect light with velvety tea roses that absorb it. Contradictory elements are a necessity in my work, and I can trace my affection for opposites back to my childhood.

I grew up in central California, home of orchards of almond and peach trees, and my family was naturally involved in agriculture. My father had almond farms, and my brothers and sisters and I harvested them. But with five children and five mouths to feed, my father had a second business as a portable X-ray technician. In the 1970s, it was one of the first of its kind. He had a van outfitted with cutting-edge equipment, which he drove to rest homes to see elderly ladies who had fallen out of bed and broken a hip. Instead of the women having to be transported to the hospital, the rest homes would call my dad and he would take his X-ray services to them. Often, I'd tag along. I would sit with him in the back of the van and watch him work in the dark, carefully dipping X-ray film into developing tanks. I loved everything about the process. The precision, the timing of it all, and the skeletal, ghostlike shapes that appeared over time.

So here I am surrounded by nature. Just outside the front door—rows of citrus and almond trees; gorgeous California live oaks growing in drifts, green, gnarly, and grand; rosebushes easily reaching ten feet tall. And inside the house, my father's work: boxes of film, hundreds of dark, shadowy images of broken pelvic bones, thighbones, and ankles. And it was this strange dichotomy, this juxtaposition of lightness and darkness, life and death that has managed to creep into my visual consciousness and directly inform my aesthetic and how I compose my work today.

A graphic black-and-white checkerboard serves as the backdrop to this still life. In the foreground is an equally graphic, very "butch" begonia leaf. Caught in the middle are these fragile little snowbells. They are the first flowers to bloom in the winter and break through the cold layers of soil and snow. This composition is about the dichotomy of hard and soft, delicate and fierce. When building an arrangement and creating a composed still life, almost every choice I make is informed by my desire to play with extremes. Just look at that large and aggressive begonia leaf, protecting those precious snowbells like a bull mastiff standing vigil in front of his owner's gate.

Many of my still lifes are inspired by Dutch
and Italian paintings. Fruits and flowers are a
common theme. From the branch to the seedpod
to the fruit, I like to showcase all the stages of
plant life. There is a lot of layering, puddling,
and grouping to be had in this particular composition, giving it a bright autumnal feel. The
glossy pomegranates and clusters of artichokes
keep company with the tulips, anemones, and
bergenia leaves. Mixed in with the smooth pears
are prickly conifers and bouncy hydrangeas. It
is truly a lavish display of contrasting colors,
shapes, and textures; but what charges me most
about this opulent feast is that the entire bounty
is presented on a plain, unfinished French laun-
dry table made out of raw pine.

FLOWERS ALWAYS COME FIRST. Their shape, color, and personality take the lead and inspire an arrangement; but in this composition, the surrounding elements, like a great supporting cast, are what make these pink garden roses shine. Old weathered wood, like this paint-splattered workbench, is the perfect surface to accentuate any fluffy and soft flower, especially these just-plucked peonies and roses, so fresh and vibrant, as if Marie Antoinette had quickly pulled them from her garden and plopped them in a vase. The backdrop, a soaring seventeenth-century gilt mirror with antiqued mercury glass resting against giant shutters, brings a magical quality to the room. Is this the parlor of a posh apartment in Paris or a dusty attic? The gold frame and blue tint of the mirror, beautifully grizzled and decadent, and the arrangement, so very feminine, youthful, and pink. It is a May-December romance in full bloom. Imagine the sugary roses in a white room or sitting on a pale pink damask tablecloth. They would look ordinary. Here, among the chipped paint and the dust, they are practically blushing.

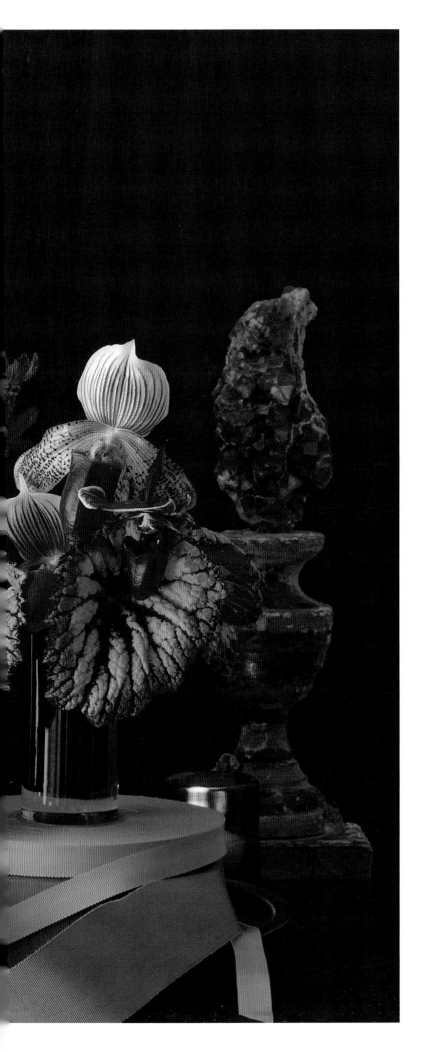

Bringing found objects into a floral composition can add dimension and interest. Here are old curiosities—an antique Italian finial, a black geode, and a wheat ornament, which typically symbolizes fertility in ancient Rome—mixed with the contemporary elements of a tightly rolled spool of green ribbon, modern votive candles, and sleek tin trays. Every object should strengthen the overall composition and look of the still life. The vibrant color of the grosgrain ribbon pulls the pale green and plum hues out of two begonia leaves, and it's as if a gnarled lilac root has scampered up to join a conversation between an eccentric lady's slipper and a clutch of muscari. Like a great dinner party, all invited guests should bring something unique to the table.

THE BEST VESSELS END UP BEING THE ONES YOU FIND—the untraditional treasures, hand thrown, intricately glazed, and won on eBay at two in the morning—and that are perhaps never even intended to hold flowers. Containers with character become an integral part of the composition. Almost all the vessels I use when creating a still life are opaque as well as unique; stems visible through a clear glass vase scream, "Flower arrangement!" A still life is about the relationship between the flowers and their container and their surrounding environment. Use an old Chinese pot, a marble urn, or a piece of German pottery from the 1960s that is one of a kind and adds something special to the overall composition. Don't use something too recognizable or a pricey crystal that can be quickly identified. I have an aversion to working with commonly used vessels for which one swift glance can easily ascertain where it came from or who made it. When it comes to vessels, I like anonymity with a ton of personality.

This arrangement is decadent and wholly unnatural: summer flowers, hydrangeas and anemones, coexisting with springtime clematis and poppies. These are flowers that would not bloom naturally together. There is a packed, smothering feeling to the arrangement, as if the flowers know they are not meant to share company and are squirming to get free. Controlling and manipulating flowers within a still life can be perversely fun. Consider these hydrangeas in their signature nautical blue, a flower best known for adorning well-manicured front lawns of the toniest summer houses on Long Island—it's nearly impossible to shake their preppy reputation. But introduce wintery elements like this thick and heavy green velvet and a bough of grapes that hint at autumn, and the hydrangeas begin to look cold—even icy—and perfectly out of place.

When choosing containers for a still life, it feels right to select ones that are handmade. I work with my hands so I think it is important to choose vases that have a life and story behind them. Someone designed this vase. A potter's hands glazed this bowl. These are the thoughts that cross my mind when choosing containers and objects to include in my still lifes. The same applies to found objects and curiosities. A piece of driftwood, a bunch of moss or coral, even a tangle of old nautical rope— nature's weathered gems are great additions to any floral still life.

Michelangelo Merisi da Caravaggio, *John the Baptist* (1597–98)

I draw tremendous inspiration from Caravaggio's oil paintings. His compositions are sexual and raw, decadent and slightly rotten—much like this crabapple arrangement with its wormy apples, sawed-off branches, and chewed-up leaves. In this painting, the abundance and contrasts of color and texture, like the lamb's nubbly wool, the smooth skin of the young boy, and the rough leaves of the raspberry vines, create a complete picture, so balanced and nuanced. This is what I strive to achieve when working with my flowers and chosen elements.

When I am building an arrangement or creating a composed still life, every choice is informed by my desire to use dueling elements. If I am using a raw wooden table, I will drape a piece of rich velvet fabric upon it. Something rough with something polished. This jug—which looks as though it's been dredged up from the bottom of the sea, with a frayed gnarled rope wrapped and twisted around it—is paired with frothy white garden roses and hellebores. Contrast is key.

Styling nature and bringing flowers into the home are a great luxury. Flowers are the final accessory to a room and can and should change with the seasons. Consider the color of the room and the source of light when making and placing your arrangement. The frosty palette of greens, silvery blues, and pinks in this arrangement is made with poppy pods, dusty miller, thistle, and hosta blooms. Placed in a vintage matte white McCoy vase, they are the perfect addition to a modern setting.

GIO PONTI In Praise of Architecture

MOVEMENT

The first time I saw the Martha Graham Dance Company was at Lincoln Center for the Performing Arts in 2011. A friend was a dancer in the troupe. Before that performance, my only point of reference for dance had been *The Nutcracker* and the occasional ballet, so there I was, completely in the dark and uninitiated. The curtain opened and I was blown away. I ended up going back every single night that week. That's how groundbreaking, visceral, and spirited the experience was for me.

I was so inspired by how anti-ballet it all was. The dancers activated the space around them in such a raw and heavy way. The heaviness, the pounding and falling—such a stark contrast to the bouncy and spritely ballerinas I had seen in *The Nutcracker*. And it was the falling motion that impacted me and resonates with me now. How to fall deliberately, gracefully, elegantly? In this arrangement of *Fritillaria michailovskyi*, you can feel the tiny weight of each bloom and the gorgeous droop and swoop of their leaves and stems. The wispiness of these flowers and their Medusa-like green leaves sprouting up and away from the core of the arrangement give the still life balance through movement.

Martha Graham, *Letter to the World* (1940)

MARTHA GRAHAM'S STYLE OF DANCE grew from her experimentation with the elemental movements of contraction and release. I employ the same technique with my floral arrangements in order to activate them and give them vibrancy. This is necessary and works especially well when styling and composing larger arrangements. You need to enliven the still life. The most fun arrangements are ones for which you use a substantial vessel and, taking fistfuls of lilacs, let's say, or flowering branches, just drop them into the container. It's a primal feeling. Then you add the more delicate touches, the layers and the nuances. The final act is to take the entire composition in your hands and lift the flowers up and then release them back into the vessel. Where is the logic in that? You can spend so much time placing stems, positioning leaves, trying to make things visually perfect, but the arrangement might still not be at ease. So by lifting and releasing, you are allowing the flowers to do what they naturally want to do—that's how you achieve movement. It's the most incredible way to design.

MOVEMENT IS ONE OF THE MOST IMPORTANT ASPECTS OF FLOWER ARRANGING. This has always been my approach. But historically, floral design—as a profession, as a hobby, as an art form, and certainly on the most commercial level—has been devoid of movement. What do grocery store owners and some of the most posh floral and event designers have in common? Their flowers don't move. They are stiff, stifled, and frozen. Tulips tightly arranged, tied, and packed in cellophane or a glass cylinder. Bending calla lily stems into an intricate boating knot is not my idea of styling nature. I think there is such a hunger to be creative that designers manipulate and contort flowers in an extreme way; by doing so, flowers cease to be beautiful.

This manner of controlling flowers has always created a certain level of anxiety for me. Sometimes trying to be overly creative can be the death of beauty. Meaning, don't manipulate your medium—in this case, flowers—into something far removed from its original intent. This is not to say that I don't like tailored flowers. I am a firm believer in tailoring an arrangement to fit the mood or space of a room, but there must be a balance. If you have an army of garden roses standing at attention, it's important to have a wild strawberry vine swoop in and around them to prevent the composition from looking and feeling contrived.

With movement, there is only so much manipulation that can occur before it begins to feel gimmicky. This still life of strawberries and roses took me twenty minutes to make. The best ones go really fast.

ACHIEVING THE RIGHT BALANCE is crucial in every aspect of a flower arrangement. In regards to movement, you don't want random flowers flying out of a vase; you need a composition that is controlled and stylized with moments of whimsy and serendipity. Movement occurs when a maverick leaf refuses to bend to your will . . . when a branch covered in cherry blossoms searches for the table to try and support itself. Let them act according to their natures. That glorious falling motion for the sake of its own survival—celebrate that moment. Encourage it.

Movement has a lot to do with chance and the right plant material. Do not fight against the bow of a cherry branch or the wispy nature of a sweet pea. Embrace the innate curve of a tulip stem. These random and naturally occurring events will create the movement in your flower arrangements and keep them buzzing with life and energy.

We've seen calla lilies contorted to death and demoralized. It's hard to appreciate them, much less like them anymore; but look at these glorious, bodacious bombshells! With gigantic heads and unapologetic character, they splay out and have the kinetic energy of a dynamic fountain in the gardens of the Villa d'Este in Tivoli.

Never lose sight that you are working with flowers—organic, living things. These purple sweet peas vibrate. A butterfly could float between each and every stem. This is movement. They have an easy, just-plopped-in-a-vase sensibility. But narrow your eyes, and you can see the purposefulness of a few well-placed stems. Nothing is jammed into the vessel or wired or pinned. A successful composition is one that is highly composed yet looks effortless.

SHAPE

When I think about shape, I think about the year 2000 and my first job in New York City working as a floral designer. The zeitgeist at the time inspired tightly packed dome-shaped arrangements, almost always out of roses and almost always in a square glass container. Every well-known, popular floral design studio was producing this shape and this particular style. I vividly remember stepping out for my lunch breaks and passing rows of identical arrangements made of white roses, all lined up and ready to be shipped off to Condé Nast. I would think to myself, those poor, little asphyxiated arrangements. Packed so tightly and barely able to move, let alone breathe.

The nuances that go into making a unique arrangement—color, texture, mood, movement, and seasonality—aren't a consideration when building a dome-shaped arrangement with one specific kind of flower. Learning how to make this type of floral arrangement is not difficult. Serendipity is nowhere to be found. Roses are plucked of their petals to keep their centers uniform. Their stems, stripped of their leaves, are stacked together like toothpicks. Perhaps the first person to come up with packing flowers tightly into a perfectly shaped dome struck a creative chord but after that designers might as well have been manufacturing toothpaste caps or hairbrushes.

I wanted to burst out of that mold—quite literally. To create new shapes and draw outside the lines. To leave the cookie-cutter displays behind me and, most importantly, free those tight balls of roses! I wanted undulating lines. A dead petal here. A nibbled-on leaf there. I imagined creating a collection of different shapes injected with whimsy and grace. So when I went out on my own and started LMD, that is exactly what I did.

There are four shapes that I continuously return to when working with flowers. These are the Crescent, the Sphere, the Y, and the Hogarth Curve. When considering all the makings of a floral still life it is essential to remember that shape and movement go hand in hand.

THE SPHERE

THE SPHERE HAS A SIMILAR SHAPE TO THE DOME. The trick is to create the overall shape but still break up the silhouette so it does not look static. You can achieve this by making sure you have a few renegade flowers in the mix that pop up and break the arc of the sphere. With this planetary arrangement of cherry-colored carnations, there is a consistent amount of rebellious blooms aching to break free from the pack. Those rule breakers, the ones that don't want to conform, give the arrangement life and electricity. Like sheet music, the juvenile carnation buds on the edge of the sphere act like notes dancing up and down a scale.

Without the coiling ivy, this aging wooden basket full of crimson anemones runs the risk of seeming ordinary. These blooms are chipper and perky, like a bunch of teenage carolers huddled outside your front door about to burst into a holiday jingle, but then the ivy turns the whole thing into a real symphony. Like Saturn's rings, the swooping motion of the ivy loops your eye up and around the entire arrangement—activating the space around the fluffy anemones and making the arrangement a lyrical event full of energy and excitement.

THE Y

THE Y IS AN UNUSUAL FORM THAT EXUDES STRENGTH AND AUTHORITY. I believe the Y shape was my subconscious response to the ubiquitous dome-shaped arrangements I had to make in my past—my professional and personal answer to them. How do I create a large composition using the big, voluptuous flowers that I find irresistible but also show control and movement? What I like about the Y is that it has a low, thick center, almost muscular, teeming with flowers and plant life, and then two extended arms reaching out as if to give someone a hug. Y-shaped arrangements also give you an opportunity to showcase the more botanical aspects of plant life. This particular arrangement and many of the Y-shaped arrangements I make are directly inspired by Michelangelo's male sculptures. Using juicy and feminine English garden roses, I am able to carve out hearty, generous shapes that dip, soar, and flex. Equal amounts of passion and restraint need to be exhibited in order for the Y to look controlled and not messy.

Michelangelo Buonarroti, *Prisoner or Captive known as Atlas* (circa 1516) for the tomb of Pope Julius II

THE HOGARTH CURVE

THE HOGARTH CURVE is an S-shaped line appearing within an object. In this case, the serpentine line is made with dahlias and peonies. Eighteenth-century English artist William Hogarth believed that a curved line signifies liveliness and stimulates the attention of the viewer, in contrast with a straight line that signifies stasis and death. I love the Hogarth Curve because the shape reminds me of a wave that swells in the middle of the ocean. These peonies and dahlias are natural sun worshippers, meaning their heads instinctively angle upwards. Using their natural urges, I was able to create one seamless, undulating line.

There is something very painterly about Hogarth Curve arrangements. Use sumptuous flowers—begonias, anemones, peonies—and the natural shape of their stems to help create ebbs and flows within a composition. In this arrangement a dollop of begonias touches the fireplace mantel, their curved stems bending naturally under their own glorious weight.

When snipping a flower or taking blossoms out of their packaging, take the time to examine their stems and the way their leaves spring or heads droop. Use their innate predilection to your advantage. Many flowers have tons of personality. Poppies and anemones have twisty stems—follow those lines and employ them to assist you in the shape you are trying to create. Mesmerizing shapes can occur by simply letting the flowers do the work. These water lilies are a perfect example of the most organic, nailed-it-didn't-do-a-darn-thing-to-them floral arrangement. Sometimes magic happens by just introducing the right flowers to the right vessel.

THE CRESCENT

THE SWEEPING SHAPE OF THE CRESCENT appeals to me for many different reasons. The elastic arc reminds me of an outstretched dancer's back, or the magnificent domed ceilings of the Hagia Sophia. With flowers like these German bearded irises, the Crescent resembles a metronome keeping time, each lithe stem symbolizing the fluid movement of the metronome's needle. The repetition, symmetry, and rhythmic qualities of the Crescent are so visually appealing to me. I have a strong affinity for all things Roman and the shape of the Crescent corresponds to the prominent arches of the Coliseum and Rome's impressive aqueducts. I love how you can take a shape that is extremely masculine and powerful and, by using flowers, turn it into a soft and inviting silhouette.

Louis Haghe, *Interior of the Hagia Sophia in Constantinople transformed into a mosque* (1850)

Crescent-shaped arrangements echo
the form of a waning moon. Astrology
interests me and I have many moons in
my birth chart so perhaps I am drawn to
the Crescent for celestial reasons.

It is important to remember that the silhouette of an arrangement will change over time. An arrangement is a living thing; by day three the flowers will have taken on a new shape. Many admirers and consumers of flowers abhor this process; they think it happens too quickly instead of surrendering to how beautiful the evolution can be. To witness a flower open and, in time, collapse is wonderful. There are certain kinds of flowers—tulips, hyacinths, and anemones, for example—that will continue to grow well after they are cut. When plants and flowers are almost on the verge of collapse, this is when they are the most beautiful to me. Tulips are great shapeshifters; they die so beautifully. The blossoms begin in the shape of an egg and then each petal stretches and opens wide before it falls away.

TEXTURE

A lot of my work could be viewed as heavy-handed. I am a sucker for big, flowery flowers, the juicier and fluffier the better. Roses, peonies, ranunculi, and anemones—I use them in arrangements often and with great joy. This is clearly my feminine side at work, my adoration for bouncy, floppy blooms. But my masculine side always feels compelled to toughen up the end result, and this is where texture comes into play.

Overtly masculine responses to pretty, round flowers like roses and peonies come in the form of any fruiting branch: privet berries do the trick with their dark blue, smooth, wonderfully glossy fruits that resemble clumps of miniature champagne grapes. Fig and olive work well with their slender branches and stiff leaves. Herbs, thistle, and most tree foliage—Chinese pistachio, plum branches, and acacia leaves—provide great contrast to fluff.

Texture can be introduced into an arrangement in one of two ways, either with flowers, berries, and textured foliage or with the choice of vase.

Julian Schnabel, *Portrait of Lola* (1996)

These dinner-plate dahlias in shades of grapefruit resemble sunbursts. With their comparatively dark centers and layers of flame-tipped petals, they are a textural flower in their own right. Further texture is introduced with hanging bunches of tender hypericum berries. But the most flagrant textural interplay is between the flowers and the vessel they are placed in. This sculptural ceramic bowl—with its deep, scar-like grooves and dark bronzed patina—looks almost volcanic in nature. And then, leaping out of it are these chipper dahlias, so bright and happy. The brazen juxtaposition of these two elements is so satisfying; it is a true mix of feminine and masculine, perfectly aligned.

This arrangement is an exemplary study in texture. Look at the contrast between the flowers and the container—a glazed ceramic cube with a crackled finish. Pouring out of its hard edges are furry elements that drip and move and creep and crawl. The arrangement looks like a creature that lives at the bottom of a swamp. But none of these plants is aquatic; the composition consists of fern fronds, begonia leaves, amaranthus, and the common garden zinnia.

There is magic in these Icelandic poppies. The life cycle of a poppy is very textural. When not fully opened, their blossoms resemble tadpoles. In full bloom, their petals are as transparent as gossamer silk, their stems covered in what looks like soft peach fuzz. Placed in a voluptuous, gourd-shaped Astier de Villatte vase with fragrant juniper boughs crowning the base, this composition is a fine representation of tactility.

Sweet peas are typically pegged as delicate, darling flowers but in this arrangement they look crunchy, leathery, and downright stubborn. Their actual petals are tissue thin and stand in direct contrast with the rough, thick skin of the beet in the foreground of the still life. The flowers are the largest component in this composition and they are breathtaking. But if you take in all the other surface elements—the texture of the beet's skin against the shiny bergenia leaf that is wrapped around the vessel and the matte lead plate with the prickly cedar coming into focus—it's all of these other moments happening around the sweet peas that create a multilayered and highly tactile event. These elements are the most interesting part of this still life; the whole in this case is greater than the sum of its parts.

I don't work with tropical or subtropical plants and flowers very often. But I couldn't resist the prehistoric-looking flora in this arrangement. When using tropical flowers, my style is to keep true to their Jurassic nature. What inspired this arrangement were the acid-yellow mimosa blooms, the texture of the caterpillar-like wild fern that releases a silver tint, and the giant spindly protea flowers that resemble overgrown pincushions. I stay away from the kinds of tropical plants that everyone uses like banana palms and bird-of-paradise. Unexpected pairings excite me.

PAGES 2–3: Hyacinth, hydrangea, tweedia, corylus, passionflower vine, blue eryngium

PAGE 4: Camellia foilage, seeded hedera, umbrella fern, tree peony

PAGE 6: Chrysanthemum

PAGE 9: 'Coral Charm' peony, fuchsia, grape ivy

PAGE 10: Rhododendron, lilac, allium, 'Romantic Antike' garden rose, eggplant, single petal ranunculus

PAGES 14–15: Dahlia

PAGE 17: Ranunculus, crespidia, sweet gum, cymbidium orchid, 'Capriccio' garden rose, 'Free Spirit' garden rose

PAGE 18: Rose hip, begonia foliage, sedum, scabiosa pod, passion fruit vine, cotinus, purple basil, American chestnut

PAGES 20–21: Chokecherry, coleus, maple, sarracena

PAGE 22: Umbrella fern, Japanese spray rose, 'Green Trick' dianthus, hellebore, ranunculus, allium

PAGE 25: Purple basil, scabiosa, angelica, 'Purple Majesty' millet

PAGES 26–27: Purple basil

PAGE 29: Dahlia, heuchera foliage

PAGES 30–31: Red horse chestnut, honeysuckle, 'Juliet' garden rose, spray rose, anemone

PAGES 32–33: Scented geranium, eucalyptus, sweet pea, ranunculus, passionflower vine, parrot tulip, 'Kansas' peony

PAGE 34: Hydrangea, hybrid delphinium, clematis, hyacinth, eryngium

PAGE 35: Viburnum berry, *Fritillaria persica*, black ammi, carnation, delphinium, hyacinth, fern, ivy, epidendrum orchid, spirea, variegated euonymous

PAGES 36–37: Poppy, kumquat, photinia, genista

PAGE 39: 'Maria Theresa' garden rose, ranunculus, dahlia, acacia foliage, callistemon

PAGE 40: Ranunculus, poppy, scented geranium, eucalyptus, double lisianthus, calamondin

PAGE 41: *Hydrangea paniculata*, 'Romantic Antike' garden rose, garden rose, dahlia, begonia, passionflower vine, angelica, corylus, belladonna lily

PAGES 42–43: Rose, eucalyptus

PAGES 44–45: *Fritillaria imperialis*, peony, amaryllis, poppy, tulip, ranunculus, sweet pea, scented geranium

PAGES 46–47: Dahlia, begonia, hop bine, ranunculus, tulip, viburnum berry

PAGES 48–49: Lilac, campanula, *Pieris japonica*, rhododendron, tulip, *Trifolium rubens*

PAGE 50: Acacia, eucalyptus, ranunculus, lemon

PAGES 52–53: Peony, garden rose, strawberry, elderberry, viburnum, ranunculus, potato vine

PAGE 55: Rex begonia, snowbell

PAGES 56–57: Hydrangea, seeded hedera, pear, pomegranate, anemone, ranunculus, sweet pea, artichoke, peony, pine, tulip, ivy, bergenia, cedar

PAGE 59: Peony, garden rose, strawberry, elderberry, ranunculus, potato vine

PAGES 60–61: Muscari, Rex begonia, lady slipper's orchid, lavender

PAGE 62: Nigella, corylus

PAGE 65: Hydrangea, poppy, clematis, *Fritillaria meleagris*, peony, garden rose, anemone, Rex begonia, leucocoryne

PAGES 66–67: Bergenia, geranium, fern, hedera, viburnum, porcelain berry, trachillium

PAGE 69: Olive, carnation, eucalyptus, 'Toulouse-Lautrec' garden rose

PAGES 70–71: Crabapples

PAGE 73: Spray rose, hellebore, eryngium, lilac

PAGES 74–75: Dusty miller, hosta bloom, garlic chive flower, white eryngium, poppy pod, aspalathus, heuchera bloom, *Geum triflorum*, grass

PAGE 76: Ranunculus, eucalyptus, 'Alabaster' garden rose, hellebore, pussy willow

PAGE 77: Paperwhite, poppy, pomegranate

PAGES 78–79: Rex begonia, blackberry, sweet pea, allium, scabiosa

PAGE 81: *Fritillaria michailovskyi*

PAGES 82–83: Clematis, hellebore, tuberose, passionflower, cymbidium orchid

PAGE 84: Geranium, plumosa fern, jasmine, scabiosa, Mokara orchid, hedera, black philodendron, *Clover lindera*

PAGES 86–87: Peony, cherry blossom, chrysanthemum

PAGE 89: Osteospermum, Rex begonia

PAGES 90–91: Rose 'François Rabelais' garden rose, hellebore, tomato, strawberry, nigella

PAGES 92–93: Lilac, coleus, ixia, caladium, ranunuculus, photinia, osteospermum, hellebore

PAGE 94: Ranunuculus, heuchera foliage

PAGES 96–97: Ixia, clematis, tulip, lamb's ear, geranium, garden rose, petunia

PAGE 98: Calla lily, salix, asplenium

PAGES 100–101: Anemone, geranium, fern, scabiosa, berzillia

PAGES 102–103: Japanese tree peony, dahlia, asclepia, trollius

PAGE 105: Sweet pea, leucocoryne

PAGES 106–107: Azalea, crabapple, narcissus, geranium

PAGES 108–109: Blackberry, German bearded iris, cornflower, calla lily, potato vine, coleus

PAGE 110: Hosta, hop bine, passionflower vine, hydrangea, 'Green Trick' dianthus, northern sea oat

PAGES 112–113: Peony, rhododendron, blueberry, dianthus, sweet pea, hosta

PAGE 114: Sunflower, tansy, viburnum berry, dahlia, rudbeckia

PAGE 115: Hellebore, ranunculus, *Fritillaria elwesii, Fritillaria meleagris, Fritillaria raddeana, Fritillaria persica*, parrot tulip, hedera

PAGE 116: Carnation

PAGE 119: Anemone, privet, ivy

PAGES 120–121: Cosmos

PAGE 122: 'Toulouse-Lautrec' garden rose, hellebore, Korean spicebush, ivy

PAGES 124–125: Dahlia, amaranthus, mountain mint, cotinus, hydrangea, burning bush, crabappple, garden rose, Rex begonia, echinacea pod

PAGE 126: *Fritillaria persica*, 'Buckeye' peony, dahlia, Japanese painted fern, parrot tulip, coleus

PAGES 128–129: Dahlia, viburnum

PAGES 130–131: Peony, Solomon's seal, maidenhair fern, hellebore, lilac, sweet pea, hosta

PAGES 132–133: Begonia, sweet pea, artemisia

PAGE 135: Water lily

PAGE 136: German bearded iris, rose foliage

PAGES 138–139: Lily of the valley, viola

PAGES 140–141: Miniature gladiolus

PAGES 142–143: Lily, 'Tess' garden rose, hellebore, spirea, ranunuculus, photinia, scabiosa, *Fritillaria persica*

PAGES 144–145: Parrot tulip, sweet pea

PAGES 146–147: Queen Anne's lace, pear, porcelain berry

PAGE 148: 'Combo' rose, dusty miller, Rex begonia, berzillia, variegated Italian pittosporum, skimmia

PAGES 150–151: Sunflower, berzillia, sumac

PAGES 152–153: Dahlia, hydrangea, crabapple

PAGE 154: Ranunculus, fig, dill, *Fritillaria persica*, *Fritillaria meleagris*, passionflower vine, artichoke, isopogon

PAGE 155: Garden roses, scabiosa pod, olive, ligustrum, sunflower, cymbidium orchid, hellebore foliage

PAGES 156–157: Crabapple, 'Juliet' garden rose, peppermint

PAGES 158–159: Allium, anemone, hyacinth, fern, geranium

PAGES 160–161: Amaranthus, zinnia, scabiosa pod, Rex begonia, fern frond

PAGE 162: Ligustrum berry, hydrangea, anemone, *Cumosum leucodendron*

PAGE 163: Sunflower, dahlia, purple basil, begonia, lily, scabiosa

PAGES 164–165: Clematis, scabiosa, potato vine, blackberry, bachelor button, iris

PAGES 166–167: 'Majolika' spray rose, O'Hara garden rose, raspberry, anemone, hellebore, viburnum, leucojum, sweet pea, Solomon's seal

PAGES 168–169: Icelandic poppy, juniper, cedar

PAGES 170–171: Chrysanthemum

PAGE 172: Sweet pea, bergenia, Blue Atlas cedar

PAGES 174–175: Lady's slipper orchid, Rex begonia, corylus, ligustrum

PAGES 176–177: Dahlia, rose hip, amaryllis, wild smilax vine

PAGE 179: Mimosa, ranunculus, pincushion protea, grevillea, Australian curly pine, fern, colocasia

ACKNOWLEDGMENTS

I would like to express my sincere gratitude to the people who have continuously supported me and LMD. I would also like to thank everyone who has contributed to this book.

To my dear friend Don Freeman. We have been working together for over a decade—it has been the most satisfying and rewarding experience. I hope we continue to create beautiful, lasting still lifes together for many years to come.

To Philip Reeser, my editor, for keeping us all on task and for understanding the vision and direction. And my gratitude to Charles Miers, publisher at Rizzoli, and Phil Kovacevich, the book's designer.

To my friend Irini Arakas: from day one, you had me with your style, talent, wit, and humor, mixed with that perfect urban edge—you bring my voice to life.

To those who have kindly allowed us to shoot on their property: Ron Sharkey, The Black Barn, High Falls, New York; Andrea J. Filippone, Jardin de Buis, Pottersville, New Jersey; Anouk Beerents, Antieke Spiegels, Amsterdam. And my buddy Rutger Mulder and Janny "Shirley" Mulder for letting us invade their house and garden.

To my staff—Team LMD. The most amazing group of people in the world. I could not ask for a better group of creative professionals with whom to work, laugh, and create beauty… your dedication, talent, and professionalism make me speechless.

To all of the event planners with whom I work (in alphabetical order!)—Francesca Abbraccamento, Alimay Events, Elizabeth Allen, Vivia Costalas, Leslie Mastin, Leslie Price, Maria Seremetis, Eyal Tessler, Loulie Walker, Jennifer Zabinski, and many more. Your constant support, friendship, belief, and trust in LMD are what keep us going.

To my suppliers—Dutch Flowerline, G. Page, George Rallis, J&P Flowers, 28th Street Flowers, Associated, US Evergreen, and my very favorite buddy, lifesaver, and champion of all, Louie at Major Wholesale. Even now I find myself at the market at least three mornings a week. It's the best way to start the day.

To my bestie, Oliver Tobin: our all-night conversations about life, art, and Madonna are some of my very favorite things. I love you.

To Laura Seita, my friend, confidante, and horticultural encyclopedia. You are everything to me. Thank you for being there for me in so many ways. You've seen it all.

To Russell Labosky, for believing in me, pushing me, and teaching me to never, ever give up.

And lastly, to my loving and supportive family, thank you.

I dedicate this book to my grandparents: Hubert and Mildred Miller, and David and Sarah Lee Switzer.